A COMPLIMENTARY REVIEW COPY, SPRING 1970

A DEFENDERS OF FREEDOM BOOK

John J. Pershing: World War I Hero

BY JOHN FOSTER
ILLUSTRATED BY HERMAN B. VESTAL

ABOUT THE BOOK: Here in colorful detail is the story of John J. Pershing who, after a lifetime of military service, received the highest rank ever given to an American soldier—General of the Armies. The courage and dignity, even in the face of personal tragedy, that marked Pershing's brilliant leadership of the American Forces in World War I, reveal a man who lived by his West Point Creed of "Duty, Honor, Country." This is one of Garrard's DEFENDERS OF FREEDOM books, which feature the life stories of fascinating characters, both contemporary and historical, and reconstruct with detail and action many of the important crises in history.

Subject classification: Social Studies, American History, Biography
Sub-classification: World War I, Military History, Reading, Information

ABOUT THE AUTHOR: John Foster's work on newspapers in Florida, North Carolina, New York, and Louisiana won him two Associated Press awards for journalism. He is presently the editor of *Dawn*, the weekend magazine of the *Suffolk Sun*. Mr. Foster has traveled widely through the United States, the Central Pacific, and Japan, where he was a marine in the Second World War. When he is not working, Mr. Foster likes to swim and go on long walks with his dog, Count, in the hills near his home in Huntington, Long Island, where he lives with his wife and two children. This is his second book for Garrard, following *Sir Francis Drake*.

Reading Level: Grade 5   Interest Level: Grades 4–7
112 pages . . . 6⅞ x 9⅛   Publisher's Price: $2.69

SBN 8116-4603-3

Illustrated with photographs and 2-color art; full-color jacket; reinforced binding; index

GARRARD PUBLISHING COMPANY

JOHN J.
PERSHING

World War I Hero

JOHN J. PERSHING

World War I Hero

BY JOHN FOSTER

ILLUSTRATED BY HERMAN B. VESTAL

GARRARD PUBLISHING COMPANY
CHAMPAIGN, ILLINOIS

For another John, my son,
in hopes that the life story
of this great American will be
an inspiration to him.

J
923.5
P

Contents

1. Head of the House

"Come on, girl!" Fourteen-year-old John J. Pershing urged his horse forward. The big bay stretched out her legs, hoofs drumming on the red clay road. John enjoyed riding more than any other sport, and he and the bay moved gracefully together.

The green countryside of Linn County, Missouri, was beautiful in the fading sunlight that warm September afternoon in 1874. John breathed deeply of the sweet air. A horse to ride, woods to hunt in, streams filled with fish—what more could a boy ask for?

When John came clopping into the yard of the Pershing farm in Laclede, his father was waiting for him on the porch. John immediately noticed his father's long face.

"What's wrong, Dad?" he asked. "Am I late for supper?"

"No, son," John F. Pershing answered gently. "I'm afraid I have bad news."

As the oldest of six children, John was used to serious conversations with his father. The two walked side by side through the yard, the boy listening gravely as the man talked.

The last sunlight of the dying day glowed on John's curly blond hair. Big for his age, he was not much shorter than his father. He was lean and straight with hard muscles and steady gray eyes.

"We're in trouble, son," Mr. Pershing said. "As you know, the whole country has been suffering from a depression. But lately things have gotten worse. I've just come from the bank. I couldn't get a loan. The store, the lumberyard—we've lost them both."

Mr. Pershing's grim words seemed to drill into the boy's head, and he looked up at his father sadly. John had never seen him so tired and discouraged.

"All we've got now is this little farm," Mr. Pershing went on. "I was lucky enough to get a job selling clothes on the road, and I leave tomorrow. That means you're the head of the house."

John swallowed. "Yes, sir," he said. Then, putting his hand on his father's arm, he added, "Don't worry, Dad. We'll make out somehow."

The next few years were hard ones for the Pershings, but make out they did. John, his mother, two brothers, and three sisters ran the farm with no outside help. Mr. Pershing came home for short visits when he could.

Besides his other chores, John did all the plowing. Whenever he came to a rock, he refused to plow around it, as most farmers did. He struggled until he had forced it out of the ground.

"One thing you can say about that Pershing boy," the neighbors remarked, "his furrows are always straight."

As busy as he was, John continued his schooling. At night when all the chores were finished, he did his homework. He did not learn easily, but he studied until he knew the next day's lessons well.

Before the depression, Mr. Pershing had planned for John and the other children to go to college, but now there was not enough money. When John graduated from high school at the age of seventeen he had to get a job. He started to teach in an elementary school near his home. At that time not all teachers were required to have a college education. Mrs. Pershing and the younger children continued to work on the farm, and John helped them on weekends and vacations.

Two years later, John found a job that paid more

money. He was now teaching in a one-room school-house in Prairie Mound, Missouri, about ten miles from his home. John, nineteen, had students who ranged in age from six to twenty-one. He had difficulty with some who were as old or older than he.

One day one of the bigger girls caused a disturbance in class.

"You are to remain at your desk during lunch period," John told her.

When his back was turned, the girl climbed out of the window and ran home. The next day John again told her to remain at her desk, and he stayed in the room to be sure she obeyed. Her younger sister, also one of John's students, ran home and told their father.

That afternoon, as John was teaching a class, he heard the pounding of hoofs. Looking out the window, he saw a man with a red beard galloping up the road, carrying a shotgun.

As the horseman thundered into the schoolyard, John picked up a poker from the iron stove that heated the room and walked out onto the front steps.

"I'm taking my daughter home!" the man shouted, jumping off his horse.

"Shoot him!" the girl yelled from the window. "Shoot him, Pa!"

"No!" the other students screamed. They liked their teacher, who was strict but fair.

John took a firm grip on the poker and started toward the man. "You may shoot me, sir," he said quietly, "but that is the only way you'll get your daughter out of school before the end of class."

"Shoot him, Pa!" the girl yelled again. "I want to go home!"

Slowly, her father raised the shotgun, aiming it at John's chest. John took a deep breath. Nobody spoke. The horse snorted, pawing the ground. The white-faced students watched from the windows.

At last the bearded man lowered his shotgun and, without a word, jumped back on his horse and galloped away. His daughter stayed in school until the end of class. She came back the next morning as if nothing had happened.

John enjoyed teaching, but he wanted a college education. He saved some of the money he earned and attended the state's teacher-training school at Kirksville during two spring terms in 1879 and 1880. He still did not feel that he was an educated man.

One day when he was twenty-one, a newspaper story caught his eye. It announced competitive examinations for the United States Military Academy at West Point, New York.

"I'm going to take the tests," he told his mother.

She looked up at him with tears in her eyes. "But, John, you're *not* going to be a soldier, are you?"

"Mother," he said softly, "this way I can get a free college education. Cadets have permission to resign from the army upon graduation if they care to. I might do that and come home to study law."

John took the examinations and won an appointment to West Point. At the Military Academy he soon realized that he wanted the life of a soldier. The rules were strict and the training was hard, but he enjoyed discipline. He had governed himself strictly since he was fourteen.

The classwork was difficult for him, but he studied hard.

"Oh, come on, John!" his roommate would exclaim. "It's Saturday night! Everyone else is having fun — and you just sit there with that old French book!"

"I'm not getting up from this table until I know my assignment," John answered.

"You're turning into a bookworm," his roommate said. "I've seen you go without meals so you could study. It's just not worth all that!"

"It is to *me*," John quietly replied and went on studying.

Because of his serious nature, John was not especially popular with his classmates. But they saw that he was a natural leader and in his senior year elected him captain of cadets.

What John enjoyed most at West Point, besides

West Point Cadet, John J. Pershing, Class of 1886.

horseback riding, were the military activities — guard duties, inspections, and parades. He considered it a special honor to be able to salute the great Union general of the Civil War, William T. Sherman, who often visited the Military Academy.

General Sherman handed out the diplomas when John's class graduated in June, 1886. One by one, the seniors strode forward as their names were called, saluted, and were handed their parchment scroll.

"Second Lieutenant John J. Pershing!"

John marched to the platform, saluted General Sherman for the last time and received his diploma.

"Good luck, Lieutenant," the old General said.

"Thank you, sir," John replied, shaking his hand.

When the last name had been called, the band started to play, and long formations of cadets marched past the graduating class in review, flags fluttering in the breeze. John, however, was scarcely aware of anything but the diploma clutched in his hand. He was a second lieutenant in the United States Army!

2. Indian Trouble

For his branch of the service, Lieutenant Pershing chose the cavalry, then the most exciting duty in the army.

He was ordered to the Sixth Cavalry Regiment at Fort Bayard, New Mexico, a lonely post near the Mexican border. When Pershing reported for duty, the regiment was fighting a group of Apaches in one of the nation's last Indian wars. The hostile Apaches were led by their fiery chief, Geronimo.

Pershing was assigned the dangerous task of taking supplies to isolated army posts in the Apache country. He and a detail of horsemen accompanied a train of mules that carried food, water, and ammunition through the desert.

"Sir, look!" his sergeant exclaimed, pointing to a series of gray puffs of smoke that arose from a distant hill. "Smoke signals!"

"Yes, the Apaches are watching every move we make," Pershing replied. "We'll never catch them napping."

He and his men had many sharp clashes with the enemy, but he came to admire the Indians—both friendly and hostile.

From Apache scouts Pershing gradually learned to speak the Apache language.

Following sixteen months of bitter combat, Geronimo and his warriors surrendered to the army. An uneasy peace settled upon the land.

After two years at Fort Bayard, Pershing was sent to nearby Fort Stanton. One hot morning a message arrived, saying that three white men had stolen some horses from a Zuni camp. The Indians had chased the trio to a ranch house, which the whites had turned into a fort.

"This could be serious," Pershing's commander told him. "If we don't handle it right, we could have another Indian war on our hands. Take a detail and bring those horse thieves in."

Pershing and ten cavalrymen galloped off into the

desert, taking with them a horse-drawn wagon. As his little column drew near the ranch house, Pershing could hear the sharp angry popping of gunfire.

Leading his men up a steep hill, he counted more than a hundred Indians on the hilltop. Crouched behind rocks, they were firing at the small ranch house in the valley below. Puffs of smoke appeared at the windows and bullets buzzed through the air as the whites returned the fire.

When Pershing and his men rode over to the Indian chief, the enraged braves crowded around them, aiming their rifles. One word from the chief, Pershing knew, and he and his men would be dead.

"Put down your arms," he ordered quietly. "We have come to arrest those men."

"No!" the braves shouted, taking fresh aim.

"Never!" the chief announced. "They stole our horses and killed three of my warriors. We want them dead or alive!"

"Those men are American citizens," Pershing said. "We will punish them ourselves."

The battle continued while Pershing and the chief argued. The chief was firm, but Pershing was more firm. At last the Indian leader signaled to his braves to stop firing. Pershing rode down to the ranch house and hammered on the bullet-splintered door with the butt of his revolver.

From inside came a rumble as furniture was dragged back. Slowly the door opened, and a man with a bloody handkerchief around his head peered out. His face was pale, and his hands were shaking.

"I've come to take you in," Pershing said.

"Not on your life!" the man cried. "As soon as we set foot outside, those redskins will shoot us down!"

"No, they won't," Pershing said. "My soldiers and I will protect you."

"Yah!" the man sneered. "They'll shoot you down, too. They've got ten men for every one of yours."

"Do as I say!" Pershing commanded.

The three men inside the house held a frightened conference and decided that they had no choice but to do as Pershing said. Pershing called his soldiers, who came down the hill with the wagon. The three men climbed into the wagon, and Pershing stationed his cavalrymen around it.

"Forward!" he commanded. Quietly he told his men, "Don't shoot unless they fire first."

The tiny force rode up the hill toward the Zunis, who waited silently until the wagon and its escort reached them. Then the Indians broke into wild screams. Running alongside the wagon, they tried to slip through the cavalrymen to get to the cringing horse thieves. Pershing spotted a score of rifles leveled at him alone.

"Keep going," he ordered his men. "Keep going—no matter what!"

For a frantic period it looked as though the Zunis would overwhelm them, but neither side opened fire, and Pershing led his group safely back to Fort Stanton. There the three men were locked in the guardhouse to stand trial for their crimes.

In recognition of his expert handling of the dangerous situation and for his leadership, Pershing was given command of a cavalry troop.

"He's a tough, demanding officer, but I'm proud to be serving under him," one of his soldiers remarked to a buddy.

Lt. Pershing (first row, fourth from left) at Fort Bayard with other officers and their families.

"He seems a lot more interested in his men than most other officers are," the other soldier replied. They knew that Pershing always saw that his soldiers had good food, clean living quarters, and plenty of feed and water for their horses.

The commanding officer of the Sixth Cavalry Regiment summed up Pershing's fitness report with these words: "Professional ability, most excellent; capacity for command, excellent."

In 1891, when Pershing was thirty-one years old, he was sent to the University of Nebraska in Lincoln as professor of military science and tactics. He found the corps of cadets there to be an untrained, lazy group. But, enforcing the iron discipline he had learned at West Point, Pershing soon had a drill team that won many awards. During his second year at Nebraska he was promoted to first lieutenant.

After four years at the university, he returned to active duty at Fort Assinboine in Montana, where he was given command of a troop in the Tenth Cavalry. The Tenth was a crack regiment of Negro troops. They had been campaigning against the Indians since the regiment was formed shortly after the Civil War.

Their current assignment was to round up a party of 600 renegade Cree Indians. The Crees had slipped across the border from Canada and were attacking isolated American ranches.

Pershing always felt a special pride in the courage of
the Tenth Cavalry, shown here in action.

The Indians were valiant fighters and fine horsemen, but the black soldiers proved themselves to be
superior in all respects. They rounded up the Crees,
then escorted them back across the border. During
the brief campaign, Pershing formed a high respect
for the fighting ability of black soldiers.

The following year he was ordered to army
headquarters in Washington, D.C., as aide to the
general in chief of the U.S. Army, Nelson A. Miles.
The new position was an honor and the first important
step upward in Pershing's career.

One evening General Miles sent Pershing to
observe a military tournament in Madison Square

Garden in New York City. There Pershing met Theodore Roosevelt, at the time city police commissioner.

"I've heard fine things about you, Lieutenant," Roosevelt said in his reedy voice as they shook hands.

"And I've heard the same about *you*, sir," Pershing replied with a grin.

He liked Roosevelt's firm grasp and the steady eyes that flashed behind the rimless spectacles. At thirty-eight, Teddy Roosevelt was just two years older than Pershing. He was a wiry man, and every movement showed his great enthusiasm and fierce energy.

As they watched the military units going through their maneuvers in the arena below, the two men engaged in a lively conversation. They had much in common. Both were firm believers in physical fitness. Both were excellent horsemen. Both had spent years in the West and knew the Indians, whom they regarded highly.

At Madison Square Garden that evening, the two men formed a lasting friendship. The meeting proved later to be an extremely fortunate one for Pershing, for Roosevelt was to become an important person in government.

Pershing's next post was as an instructor at the United States Military Academy. The cadets, who thought he was too strict even by West Point standards, resented him and tried to think of uncomplimentary nicknames for him. Among themselves, the cadets began to refer to Pershing as "Black Jack."

Pershing was walking down the hall to class one day when he saw a tall cadet duck into the room and heard him whisper, "Quiet, here comes Black Jack!"

Striding into the hushed classroom, Pershing called the tall cadet forward. "You call me 'Black Jack,'" he said, his eyes boring into the cadet's. "Why?"

The cadet was standing at rigid attention, but he could not manage his chin—it quivered. "Well, sir, uh," he stammered, "it's because, sir, uh . . ."

"Because I commanded black troops—right?"

"Sir, uh, yes, sir."

The roomful of cadets was even quieter than before as they awaited the explosion. Then Pershing broke into a broad grin.

"I take that as a real compliment," he said. "The Tenth Cavalry is one of the best outfits in the U.S. Army, and I'll always be proud to call it 'my' regiment."

Pershing's nickname quickly spread. Many people who were unaware of the real story thought that the name referred to his forceful personality, since a blackjack is a short leather-covered club. For the rest of his life Pershing was known to the public as "Black Jack."

3. The Charge Up San Juan Hill

For many years, diplomatic relations between the United States and Spain had been strained. While Pershing was an instructor at West Point, the tension reached the snapping point.

Cuba, an island in the West Indies, was a colony of Spain. The United States was concerned that a foreign power owned land so close to her shores. Also, Americans were angry at the cruel way the Spaniards treated their colonists.

The Cubans had risen up again and again against their rulers, but each time the Spaniards had harshly put down the revolts. Many Americans wanted to free Cuba from Spanish rule.

In February, 1898, a huge blast shook the harbor at Havana, shattering windows for miles around. The explosion was aboard the American battleship, USS *Maine*, then on a friendly visit to Cuba. The *Maine* burst into flames and quickly sank, taking with her 260 American seamen.

The Americans blamed the Spaniards, although the cause of the sinking has never been established. "Remember the *Maine!*" Americans shouted as the United States declared war against Spain.

Pershing immediately asked for a transfer back to his old outfit, the Tenth Cavalry. The commander at West Point sent Pershing's request on to headquarters at Washington, enclosing a note saying that he did not approve of the transfer.

Headquarters refused Pershing's request. The West Point commander tacked the request and the rejection on the bulletin board as a warning to other officers who also might try to get transferred.

Pershing was furious and now, more than ever, he wanted to get into combat. An old friend of his, G. D. Meiklejohn, was First Assistant Secretary of War. Pershing felt he could ask him for a favor. However, if he requested a transfer without going through channels, he might get into trouble with his commanding officers.

Pershing walked up and down in his small quarters,

thinking hard. He was thirty-seven years old and still only a first lieutenant. No one knew better than he that a soldier must obey his superiors, army rules, and regulations. But an officer who allowed his superiors to govern him completely might remain a lieutenant all his life. One who dared to take a chance might become a general.

Pershing smacked his fist into the palm of his other hand. He would call on Meiklejohn. This was the most important decision Pershing ever made.

Having obtained a short leave of absence, he took a train to Washington. There he jumped into a cab and headed for the War Department building. Meiklejohn was busy, but not too busy to see his old friend.

"Mr. Secretary," Pershing said at once, "I've come to ask for active duty."

"I'll try to get you assigned to headquarters," Meiklejohn replied.

"No, sir," Pershing said at once. "I must have line duty. If I don't get it, I'll resign from the regular army and join the Rough Riders." The Rough Riders was the name of a volunteer regiment of horsemen that Pershing's friend, Theodore Roosevelt, was forming.

"All right," Meiklejohn said at last, "I'll see what I can do."

"Thank you, sir," Pershing replied, shaking hands. He returned to West Point to await his orders.

One bright morning in May they finally came. Pershing tore open the big white envelope with nervous fingers. He was to report to his old outfit, the Tenth Cavalry!

Then he groaned. He had not been given command of a troop; he was to be the Tenth's quartermaster, in charge of their supplies. Pershing shrugged his broad shoulders. The job was not an exciting one, but it was vitally necessary. When the Military Academy commander saw Pershing's orders, he was angry, but there was nothing he could do about them.

Pershing left West Point to join the Tenth Cavalry at Tampa, Florida, one of the army's ports of embarkation for Cuba. When he arrived at Tampa, Pershing sadly shook his head at the great confusion.

The town was crammed with men, horses, and mules — all wandering around aimlessly. The air rang with angry commands and the terrified screams of the animals. On the waterfront, the docks were a hopeless disorder of supplies, wagons, and cannon.

As he directed his men in loading the Tenth's supplies aboard ship, Pershing studied the situation with great care. If he were ever in charge of an expedition, he would never permit matters to get into such a wretched condition.

Major General William R. Shafter, in command of the invasion of Cuba, had hardly enough ships to carry his troops. The American rifles and cannon were old-fashioned, Pershing noticed. Also, much of the food was rotten. And in spite of the soaring temperatures to be expected in Cuba, the men were dressed in hot blue-flannel uniforms.

In the summer of 1898, Pershing sailed with General Shafter's force for Cuba.

A Spanish fleet was anchored at Santiago, a port on the southern coast of the island. A United States Navy fleet lay outside the harbor. Shafter planned to make a landing near Santiago, then trap the enemy warships between his soldiers and the United States Navy.

The Americans splashed ashore a few miles east of Santiago on a strip of beach by a thick jungle area. Many of the men were still weak from seasickness, but fortunately the landing was unopposed. The Spaniards were waiting further inland behind strong positions on San Juan Hill, which guarded Santiago.

Pershing and the other American soldiers slashed their way through the jungle and on July 1 were ready to assault San Juan Hill. Pershing was assigned to the Second Squadron of the Tenth Cavalry, with orders to take the place of any officer who fell in action.

Soon after dawn the American and Spanish

artillery opened fire upon each other with great thundering roars. The enemy cannon were modern and more accurate than those of the United States. The Spanish shells came screaming down, crashing among the Americans at the bottom of the hill with fiery explosions. Many men were killed and wounded.

"Advance, advance, all units advance!" The command came rolling down the line.

The Americans gave a wild cheer and started up the green hill in the broiling Cuban sun. Pershing and the Tenth Cavalry were on the left flank. Next to them

"Teddy" Roosevelt and Rough Riders at San Juan.

were the Rough Riders, led by Colonel Roosevelt, who was waving his hat.

The men climbed with great difficulty through the high grass, occasionally pausing to shoot their rifles. The American cannon below them had to cease fire to avoid hitting their own men. But the Spanish artillery continued to rain down shells upon the attacking force.

From their trenches and stone blockhouses on the crest of the hill, the enemy soldiers kept up a deadly rifle fire. All around Pershing men were hit. Almost at once three bullets thudded into the commanding officer of Troop D. Pershing took charge of the unit.

The troop came to a dense thicket and a tangle of barbed wire. "The men can't get through, sir," a sergeant reported. "It's a solid barrier."

"Lie low," Pershing ordered the men.

He, himself, stood up and strolled along the obstacle, studying it carefully for some opening. The enemy bullets buzzed around him like wasps and kicked up the dirt at his feet. Pershing acted as though he were inspecting troops back in America, looking for an unbuttoned pocket flap.

But as keenly as he searched, he could find no way through the barrier. The American advance was in danger of failing, since the left flank could not keep up with the right. Then at last Pershing spotted

a narrow passage between the thicket and the wire.

"Follow me, men!" he yelled and led the way through. The Tenth Cavalry caught up with the other American units.

Cheering while firing their rifles, the Americans swept over the crest of the hill. The Spaniards retreated, turning constantly to shoot back.

Pershing watched proudly as the Stars and Stripes was raised over a blockhouse. Just as proudly, he watched one of his black soldiers giving a wounded Spanish officer the last drop of water from the American's own canteen.

In the battle, the Tenth Cavalry had lost one-half its officers, and one-fifth of its enlisted men had been killed or wounded. The charge up San Juan Hill made Pershing's respect and affection for the black fighting man stronger than ever.

Pershing glanced over at General Shafter. The general was 50 pounds overweight. His shirt was black with sweat, and he was so exhausted from the climb that he could not catch his breath to give orders. Pershing later wrote in his diary, "Officers must be in the best of health and vigor to stand the strain of war."

For his conduct in the battle, Pershing was awarded the Silver Star. The commander of the Tenth Cavalry, a combat-hardened veteran of the Civil War, told him,

"You were the coolest man under fire I ever saw."

Two days after the battle, the American navy destroyed the Spanish fleet when it tried to escape from Santiago harbor. A truce stopped the fighting around the city, and on July 16 the Spanish army surrendered.

The Spanish-American War was over — a great victory for the United States. The peace treaty made Cuba free. It also gave the Spanish islands of Puerto Rico in the Caribbean, as well as Guam and the Philippines in the Pacific, to America.

Like so many other American soldiers who escaped the Spanish bullets in Cuba, Pershing fell a victim to malaria. When he recovered from the disease, he was ordered to a desk job in Washington.

4. Duty in the Philippines

Pershing was soon promoted to captain and sent to the Philippine Islands. In the summer of 1902 he took charge of Camp Vicars, an important outpost on the island of Mindanao.

His orders were to make peace with the Moro tribesmen, fierce little warriors of the Mohammedan religion who hated all Christians. The Moros were determined to drive the Americans out of their country.

For hundreds of years the Moros had been fighting among themselves, with the other tribes in the Philippines, and with the Spaniards. War was a game to them. Pershing understood the Moros, for in many ways they were like the American Indians. He learned to speak and write the Moro language and studied their religious book, the Koran.

Many soldiers at Camp Vicars, however, had little sympathy for the Moros.

"The only good ones are dead ones," a sunburnt officer told Pershing. "Shall we send out patrols and storm their villages?"

"No," Pershing replied. "We'll send out letters."

"Letters!" the officer exclaimed. Then, seeing Pershing's face, he quickly added, "Yes, sir!"

Pershing wrote a polite letter in the Moro language to the chief of each village. He said the Americans wanted to be friends with the tribesmen and asked the chiefs to come as his guests to Camp Vicars.

A few accepted the invitation. They were barefoot, wearing white jackets and baggy trousers. They walked proudly, their heads bound in brightly colored turbans, and carried umbrellas as protection against the hot Pacific sun.

Their brown hands were close to their krises, long swords with sharp, wavy blades. One swipe could lop off a man's arm. Behind the chiefs came their bodyguards, carrying spears and ancient muskets.

The tribesmen and soldiers eyed each other suspiciously. One false move on either side and the camp would erupt in a bloody battle, with no hope of peace between the Moros and Americans. A tense hush stretched over the camp.

Then Pershing walked forward with a smile and his hand outstretched. The tribesmen glanced at each other in surprise. The American chief carried no weapon!

"Welcome, my friends," Pershing said in the Moro language. "Welcome to Camp Vicars."

He sat down with the chiefs at a long table, and his soldiers began to carry out huge platters of food. These held many different meats and vegetables but no pork, for Pershing knew that eating the flesh of a pig was against the Mohammedan religion.

As they ate and talked, the chiefs began to trust the American with the soft voice and the stern jaw. At the end of the feast they left, promising to talk to the other Moro leaders about becoming friends with the Americans. It appeared that Pershing would be the first white man to make peace with the tribesmen.

But the friendly chiefs failed. Some of them even lost their heads for having sat down at a table with the Americans, because most Moros considered peace talks a sign of weakness. The Moros sent word to Pershing that they would fight him to the death.

Pershing shrugged sadly, for he had no choice but to give battle. The Moro chiefs soon learned that the Americans were able to defeat them in battle.

However, they also learned that the Americans treated their prisoners well. One by one the chiefs came into Camp Vicars to surrender.

A little Moro leader with flashing eyes and a long krise scar across his cheek told Pershing in English, "Captain Pershing, you strong fighting man. I strong fighting man. You big chief and I big chief. We good friends."

Pershing became such good friends with some of the Moros that they decided to make him a *datu*, or tribal chief. He was the first American thus honored.

The ceremony took place outdoors. The Moro leaders and Pershing squatted around in a circle.

In the center a Koran rested on a grass mat. Guarding the sacred book was a white-haired Mohammedan priest whose servant held a silk umbrella to shield him from the afternoon sun.

Each chief in turn gave a speech welcoming the new *datu* into the group. Then Pershing and the others touched the Koran and, all together in the Moro language, announced:

"We solemnly swear eternal friendship, allegiance to the United States of America, and the end of warfare between our two peoples."

But Moro chiefs in the west, around Lake Lanao, refused to make peace, and in the spring of 1903 Pershing organized an expedition against them.

As he led his narrow column of soldiers into the thick jungle, he could feel dark eyes watching through the leaves. The soldiers gripped their rifles tightly, jumping at the jabber of monkeys and other jungle noises, expecting to be hit by a flight of spears at any moment. But none came, for the Moros were waiting to be attacked at their fortified villages.

After several days the Americans arrived at Fort Bacolod, one of the main enemy strongholds.

Carefully, Pershing studied the Moro position. The thick mud walls of the fort were topped by a high bamboo fence. Around the fort was a deep moat more than ten yards wide — too wide to jump.

"Cut down trees so they'll fall across the moat and make a bridge," Pershing told his engineers. "You riflemen, give the engineers covering fire."

Despite the constant Moro sniping, the engineers continued to work with their axes and saws. One after another the trees fell, crashing across the moat.

"Fix bayonets!" Pershing ordered. "Charge!"

The troops rushed across the tree bridges, shooting as they ran. From the fence came a long sputtering roar as the Moros opened fire with their muskets. Spears came flashing through the thick smoke, along with showers of poisoned darts from blow guns.

Pershing ran across the bridge and was boosted over the bamboo fence by one of his men. Inside the fort the soldiers and tribesmen were fighting hand to hand. The air rang with shots, shouts, and the wild clanging of the Moro war gongs.

A tribesman appeared from the smoke and rushed at Pershing, swinging a huge two-handed sword. A soldier leaped forward, jabbing with his bayonet, and the Moro fell dead.

The American assault line pressed onward. The howling tribesmen charged again and again, but they could not break through the hedge of bayonets. After 30 bloody minutes the battle ended with the Moros in full retreat, leaving their dead and wounded behind them.

"Take care of the wounded—ours and theirs,"
Pershing ordered. "Then set fire to the fort. I don't
want one stick left standing!"

In the next few weeks, Pershing marched and
fought his way around Lake Lanao. One by one, the
enemy villages fell to him and were left behind, a
mass of flames and smoke. Finally the last hostile
chief was subdued. Then the Moros and Americans
were able to live in peace.

Across the Pacific Ocean the American people
read of Pershing's triumphant campaign in their
newspapers. Editorial writers compared his march
with the ride of the great Confederate cavalry leader,
Jeb Stuart, around the Union army in the Civil War.
Pershing was called a "military genius."

Soon after the campaign ended, he was ordered
back to Washington, where he was greeted as the
nation's hero. One night at a dinner party, he met
Frances Warren, the daughter of Senator Francis
E. Warren of Wyoming. She was an attractive girl
with large, friendly eyes and a love of fun.

Frances was just out of college, while Pershing
was forty-three—nearly twice her age—but he fell
in love with her, and she returned his feeling.

They were married on January 26, 1905, during one
of the worst blizzards in Washington history. A
wedding guest was Theodore Roosevelt, then

President of the United States. He jumped out of his car, threw off his coat, and charged through the snow drifts to the church.

Less than a month later, Pershing and his young bride boarded a ship for Japan. The Japanese and Russians were at war, and Pershing was sent across the Pacific as a military observer. He left Frances Pershing in Tokyo and went on to the fighting front in Manchuria, a territory in eastern Asia which is now part of China.

Other countries also sent military observers. Like Pershing, these officers wanted to learn what changes had taken place in fighting techniques and how modern weapons, such as machine guns, affected combat. The Japanese, however, rarely allowed them to see more than a glimpse of the fighting. Occasionally they were permitted to watch a battle from a distant hilltop.

One day Pershing and the other observers stood on such a hill watching as the Russians prepared to make a cavalry charge. The Japanese soldiers waited quietly, standing in a deep trench that was heavily protected by machine guns. Even at that distance, their calm confidence was apparent.

The Russians came thundering across the field, flags flying, bugles blaring, sabers flashing in the bright sunlight.

"It's a fine brave sight, isn't it?" another observer remarked to Pershing.

"Yes," Pershing answered softly, and waited.

The Japanese line was silent as the enemy horsemen galloped closer. Then, all at once, the machine guns opened up with their loud chatter. The blizzard of bullets cut down the cavalrymen and their mounts long before the Russians could get close enough to use their sabers.

Bravery, Pershing saw, had nothing to do with the matter. To send horsemen against a position defended by machine guns was to send them to their death.

In September, 1905 — less than two years after it began — the Russo-Japanese War ended, a smashing victory for Japan.

The following year President Roosevelt promoted Pershing from captain to brigadier general — a jump of four grades and a most unusual honor. Pershing was ordered back to the Philippines, to be commander of Fort McKinley and, later, governor of the Moro Province.

The next years were happy ones for the Pershings. Like her husband, Frances was an excellent rider, and almost every afternoon they went for a gallop along the jungle roads. They also swam often, for their home was just twenty yards from the sea.

"Frankie, you're as much at ease in the water as you are on a horse," Pershing remarked to his wife. "I wish I could say the same for myself." Although he worked hard to improve his stroke, Pershing remained a poor swimmer.

"You should relax more in the water," Frances told him.

"I *could* relax more if you wouldn't swim out so far," Pershing replied. "I worry about you."

"There's no reason to worry, Jack," Frances said. "Nothing's going to happen to me."

By 1912, they had four children, three girls—Helen, Anne, and Mary—and a boy, Warren. All were good-looking, curly-haired youngsters. As soon as they were old enough to sit on a horse, they were taught to ride. They became fine horsemen and excellent swimmers.

Each day Pershing rushed home from his office to have some time with his children before they went to bed. When they started school, he heard them recite their lessons.

"You know, Frankie," he told his wife with a chuckle, "I feel like a schoolteacher again."

The happy times continued until the end of 1913, when Pershing and his family were ordered back to the United States. Pershing was made commander of the Presidio, an army base in San Francisco.

General Pershing, shown here with Mrs. Pershing and three of their four children.

5. Tragedy Strikes

Pershing and his wife were glad to be back in the United States after so many years away. Their children were delighted with their big, old frame house at the Presidio. Its long halls were fine for running, and it had many hiding places.

At night, when the children were asleep, Pershing and Frances talked softly in front of the crackling fire.

"I'm worried about the situation in Mexico," Pershing said. "They've had one revolution after another, and the country is in complete disorder, with rebels running wild all over the place. Some American businessmen with oil and cattle interests

47

there are demanding that the United States send in troops to pacify the country."

"Oh, Jack," Frances exclaimed, "do you think we'll go to war with Mexico?"

"Not if we keep a cool head," he replied.

In April, 1914, Pershing received orders to take two infantry regiments to Fort Bliss, in El Paso, Texas, on the Mexican border.

"We're going with you," Frances told him.

"I wish you could, Frankie," he answered. "But it's not safe there now. As soon as I'm sure there's no danger, I'll send for you and the youngsters."

During the months that followed, Pershing and his men helped to patrol the Mexican border. Pershing yearned for his family, and at night he wrote long letters to Frances, with special notes for each of the children.

Meanwhile, across the Atlantic Ocean, Europe appeared about to explode in a great war. Pershing knew that for nearly 50 years the European nations had been trying to increase their wealth and power. Each thought that the threat of force was the best way to get what it wanted. Most warlike of all was Germany, whose ruler, Kaiser Wilhelm II, made many fighting speeches.

Recently all the nations had begun to enlarge their armies and to line up on opposite sides. Russia and

France had agreed to help each other in case of war. Germany had made a similar agreement with Austria. The latter wanted to control Serbia, a small country now part of Yugoslavia. Russia signed a treaty with Serbia, promising to help if she were attacked. Although Great Britain had not signed a treaty with France and Russia, she was friendly with both countries.

"If war comes over there," Pershing remarked to an aide, "I expect that, sooner or later, America will be drawn into the fighting."

"Yes, sir."

"And I'm sure war will come. All it will take is an incident."

One afternoon late in June, Pershing rode back from an inspection of troops in the field. As he was dismounting from his horse, his aide ran up with the day's newspaper. Heavy black headlines announced:

CROWN PRINCE ASSASSINATED
EUROPE PREPARES FOR WAR

This story said that, on June 28th, the Austrian crown prince, Francis Ferdinand, and his wife were riding through the streets of Sarajevo, Serbia, when two pistol shots cracked out. Francis and his wife tumbled over dead in their carriage.

"That's the incident," Pershing pointed out grimly.

He was right. Because the assassin was a Serb, Austria declared war upon Serbia. At once, Russia began to mass her troops. In support of Austria, Germany declared war upon Russia and France.

The best way to attack France was through Belgium. On August 4, German forces stormed the little kingdom, breaking an earlier agreement Germany and Britain had made to guarantee Belgium's neutrality in case of war. Before the day was over Britain declared war upon Germany. World War I had begun.

On the Mexican border, Pershing studied the events across the sea with growing concern, for he knew that the United States was not prepared to fight a major war.

However, the trouble with Mexico had died down, and he was looking forward to the arrival of his family at El Paso. He had been fixing up a house for them.

One hot August morning in 1915, a week before his family was expected, an orderly came into Pershing's office with a telegram. Pershing glanced up from his papers.

"Read it to me," he ordered.

His orderly, who knew what the telegram said, hesitated.

"Go ahead," Pershing snapped at the young man.

His orderly took a deep breath and read aloud, "Deeply regret to inform you that your wife and three daughters died this morning in a fire at the Presidio..."

Only little Warren had survived. A Negro butler named Johnson had risked his life to rescue the boy.

Pershing did not speak. His eyes glittered and his jaw set tight. At once he left for San Francisco, where his son was being kept at the army hospital. The nurses closed the door upon them as Pershing knelt and took the six-year-old boy into his arms.

"We're all alone now, Warren," Pershing told him. "But we're soldiers, and we must be brave."

"Yes, Dad," Warren answered, trying not to cry.

Pershing knew he couldn't take care of his son alone and also handle his military duties. So he took the boy to Lincoln, Nebraska, where two of Pershing's sisters lived. They looked after Warren for the next few years.

Pershing spent a sad and lonely winter at Fort Bliss. People close to him thought he would lose his mind with grief, but, as he had said, he was a soldier — and the toughest kind. Each day he rode horseback until he was so exhausted he fell into bed. From that point of his life on, all of Pershing's love was divided between Warren and the army.

Meanwhile, trouble with Mexico flared up again.

Pershing leads his troops into Mexico in pursuit of the outlaw, Pancho Villa.

On the morning of March 9, 1916, the anti-American rebel leader, Pancho Villa, swooped down upon the little town of Columbus, New Mexico, at the head of 1000 horsemen. When they galloped off, they left fifteen dead American soldiers and civilians behind them.

The Mexican government gave the United States permission to follow Villa into northern Mexico. Pershing was put in command of the American force.

"Catch Villa if you can," Pershing's superior officer, General Frederick Funston, told him. "But at all costs you must do nothing that might get us into a war with Mexico."

"Yes, sir."

"The way things are going in Europe, we might be fighting there before long," Funston went on. "We can't run the risk of having a war on our own border at this time."

"Yes, sir."

A week after Villa's attack, Pershing crossed into Mexico with a column of cavalrymen. His force was gradually strengthened until it numbered 10,000 men. He had trucks as well as horses and mules. He also had field radio units, machine gun companies, and even airplanes for spotting the enemy. His command was the most modern expedition the United States ever had put into the field.

Pershing found northern Mexico to be a great desert, dotted with cactus and poor, mud-walled villages. Water was scarce, roads were even scarcer, and grass for the animals wasn't there at all. The colorful Villa was a hero to the Mexican people, who hid his men whenever the Americans pressed too closely.

Pershing marched his troops back and forth across northern Mexico, breaking up Villa's bands as quickly as they formed. There were several sharp clashes but never a real battle.

"General, this is no way to fight a war," an angry officer told Pershing.

"I agree," Pershing replied quietly. "The difference is that we're not at war."

"Well, we should be!" the officer exclaimed. "These people sure act like they're at war with *us*. We could have this whole mess straightened out in a week if we marched on Mexico City!"

"Those are not our orders," Pershing replied.

"Orders! What do those fools in Washington know about the situation here?"

The Thirteenth Cavalry searched in vain for Villa.

"Cool off!" Pershing snapped. "I know you are a brave man. But there's more to being a soldier than fighting."

In September, 1916, Pershing was promoted to major general. He was fifty-six years old, but he set such a pace that many younger officers and men could not keep up with him. He was lean and fit and tanned from the desert sun.

During the day, the desert was furnace hot. After the fiery sun went down, it was bitter cold. The lantern burned late in Pershing's tent each night, as he planned the next day's operations. Then he was up before dawn, walking through the camp to be sure all was well.

"Don't let the men be idle," he told his officers. "Idleness has ruined more armies than battles have."

Even from Mexico, Pershing continued to keep a close watch on the European situation. After the first big German offensive at the start of the war, no point in the battle lines on the Western Front had changed as much as twenty miles. But more than 1,000,000 soldiers on both sides had died in the fighting.

The men lived in dugouts deep in the ground and fought from trenches when not attacking. Pershing knew that the Allies, as the British and French were called, had begun to accept the "trench stalemate."

They had decided that they and the Germans were in a deadlock, and that neither side could advance without terrible losses. The only answer, the Allies believed, was to stay in the trenches and try to wear the enemy down.

"They'll never win the war like that," Pershing remarked to an aide as they were discussing the matter.

"Guess we'll have to go over there and show them how, General," the aide replied.

Pershing gazed at him thoughtfully.

The officer's statement was typical of the changing attitude of the American people toward the war. At first the United States had been strictly neutral, although American farmers and manufacturers had shipped their goods to the Allies. Then, as German submarines had torpedoed many American ships, and large numbers of American seamen were lost, sentiment had begun to change. Finally, the Germans declared that their submarines would immediately sink any American or other neutral ship found in the waters surrounding Great Britain.

The people of the United States considered the Kaiser an evil person and his men cruel barbarians. Louder and louder, the Americans were demanding that their government declare war upon Germany.

In Mexico, Pershing read of the growing pressure

in the newspapers and his dispatches. He knew the United States Government was about to give in, and he longed to be released to help prepare the nation for war. But he had his orders.

Then, in January, 1917, the army ordered Pershing to take his troops out of Mexico. Pershing had not captured Villa, but he had prevented him from attacking American soil again. More important, he had learned to handle a large body of men in a foreign land. He had also learned to combine old and new weapons and equipment. In addition, his troops were tested and tough—ready to train a large army.

On April 6, 1917, the United States declared war upon Germany. All over the nation, Americans cheered at the news. This, they thought, would be the "war to end war." They were "saving the world for democracy."

Pershing did not cheer, for he knew that many thousands of his countrymen would die in combat. But he felt that his government was entirely right in its action, and he was anxious to play an important role in the fighting.

6. The Western Front

The following month Pershing received orders to report to the office of Secretary of War Newton D. Baker in Washington, D.C.

Baker once said he could tell more about a general's ability by seeing him walk up and down a room than by studying his record. He had already seen Pershing's excellent record, and when the general strode into his office, Baker was convinced of his ability.

"General Pershing," he said, "you are to take command of the American Expeditionary Force for France."

"Thank you, sir," General Pershing replied softly.

He knew that he had received the greatest assignment ever given an American military commander. He would have to take charge of a huge business, for planning battles was only part of his task. He would have to see to the building of an army, then move it 3,000 miles across the Atlantic Ocean to France, along with all its arms and supplies. He would also have to train the troops for combat.

He realized that the United States Army had only 5,000 regular officers and even fewer reserve officers. In the entire country there were only 550 cannon, and enough ammunition to last nine hours of firing. The Americans had just 55 war planes, almost all of them too old for combat.

Pershing would have to build an army from scratch. Fortunately, the officers and men who had served under him in Mexico could help.

"I'll give you only two orders," Baker told Pershing. "One to go and one to return. The rest is up to you. But you must keep in mind at all times that the American army must fight as a single unit. Our soldiers are not to be fed into the British and French armies to replace their losses."

"Yes, sir."

"Good luck, General."

"Thank you, sir," Pershing said, shaking hands.

Neither man remarked that Pershing would need all the luck he could get for his great task.

On the foggy morning of May 28, the liner *Baltic* slipped out of New York Harbor, with Pershing and a small staff aboard. At that time the German U-boats were sinking one out of four ships in British waters, but the *Baltic* reached Britain safely.

Soon afterwards, Pershing arrived in Paris, France. When his special train pulled into the *Gare du Nord* station, a French army band struck up the "Star-Spangled Banner," and the crowd on the platform broke into wild cheers.

Stepping off the train, Pershing waved to the people, then climbed into a car. Slowly the motorcade drove off. From windows and balconies along the route, women threw flowers and confetti. Men, women, and children ran alongside the motorcade. Some climbed onto the roof of Pershing's car, and he could see their smiling, upside-down faces as they peered in the windows at him.

The cheers came rolling like thunder. *"Vive Pershing!* Long live Pershing!"

A shy man, Pershing was embarrassed by all the attention. The frantic welcome made him realize how desperate the French were. He represented the only hope they had left for victory.

Pershing made his headquarters in a small building

at 31 Rue Constantine in Paris. His home was a chateau by the Bois de Boulogne, a big park in the French capital.

Each morning he got up with the sunrise, ate two soft-boiled eggs, and drank a cup of strong, black coffee. Then he went for a gallop through the woodsy park, arriving at the headquarters — ready for work — when most Frenchmen were just waking up.

Pershing studied the map of France on his wall. The British were using all the country's northern ports and roads for the transportation of their soldiers and supplies. He would have to use France's smaller ports in the south, where there were few railroads and highways. His men would have to build hundreds of miles of roads and lay more hundreds of miles of railroad tracks to bring the American troops and equipment to the front lines.

At first Pershing wrote all the orders and cables himself. He always signed them JJP in bold block letters. Later he let his staff take over some of this work, but he always read the most important messages. Often he rewrote them to make them as short and clear as possible.

"We must have a million trained men in France by next May," he told his staff. "The French are tired of this war, and they're just barely holding their own now. They might crack if the Germans make

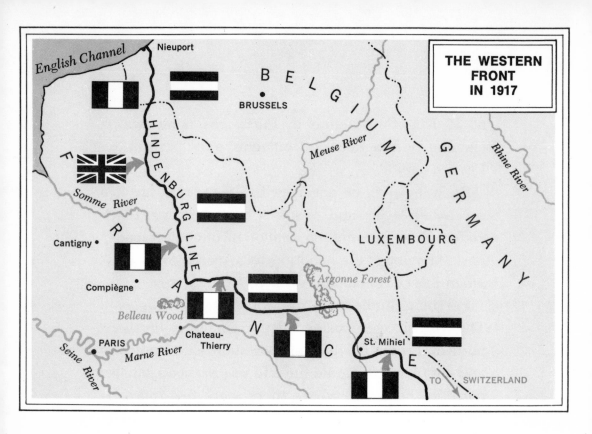

another big push next spring—which they are sure to do."

Pershing left to tour the Western Front, a line of trenches and dugouts that zigzagged for 450 miles from the English Channel to Switzerland. Pershing saw that it oozed with mud and prickled with barbed wire, while shell holes made it as pockmarked as the moon.

He was guided through the trenches to a little dugout close to the front lines, where a group of French and British officers were waiting. He could hear the distant drumming of machine guns and the occasional crash of an exploding shell as a blood-red sun set behind him.

"General Pershing, our situation is critical," a British officer told him. "The Germans have just about knocked Russia out of the war. This means that soon all the enemy divisions on the Eastern Front will be released for duty in the west. Another whole German army will crash into us."

"The Germans will take great losses," a French officer went on. "But there will be enough of them to press on to victory. That is, *Général Pershing*, unless America sends her fighting men to the trenches at once."

"The sooner we get out of the trenches," Pershing said quietly, "the sooner we win this war. We must drive the enemy out into the open and defeat him in a war of movement."

The French and British tried to hide their tired smiles. The Yankee horse soldier might know how to chase Indians and Mexican rebels, but what could he know about the fighting in Europe?

Pershing saw the look on the others' faces and knew what they were thinking. Briskly he walked over the mud floor of the dugout to the dirty map on the wall, lit up by a candle stuck in a bottle. The map showed the Western Front, marking the German and Allied positions.

Pershing pointed to a salient, a sharp wedge which the Germans had pushed into the Allied line at St. Mihiel, about 150 miles east of Paris.

"If we hit the Germans there, we could crack the whole Western Front open," he said.

"*Oui, mon général*," a French officer said. "The Americans and French fighting side by side."

"Also the Americans and British fighting side by side," a British officer said.

A German shell screamed overhead and crashed behind the dugout. Dirt rained down upon the little group. A frightened rat scurried out the doorway.

Pershing faced the other officers in the fluttering candlelight. He said softly but clearly, "Yes, we will fight with you. But we will fight as a unit, not as replacements in the French and British armies."

"But, *Général Pershing*," the Frenchman began.

"We will not argue the matter," Pershing said. "I have my orders. The Americans will fight as a unit."

Pershing returned to his headquarters. Behind him the German and Allied artillery hurled shells back and forth through the flashing, crashing night.

The troops, he thought, were living like cavemen a million years ago in their holes in the ground. This was no way to fight a war. He knew he could not change the thinking of the Allies, but he had his own ideas for the American soldier.

7. "Lafayette, We Are Here!"

On June 28, 1917, the first American soldiers landed in France. They were green troops, since Pershing had kept most of his veterans back in the United States to give each set of new recruits basic training.

Pershing watched from the pier as the Yanks, a battalion of the First Division, came off the boat and marched to their quarters. He saw that they could not keep in step and hardly knew how to carry their rifles. But they were lean and keen.

The French asked Pershing to lead the battalion in a parade through the streets of Paris on the Fourth of July. Frenchmen lining the streets shouted, "*Les Américains* have arrived!" until they were hoarse. A

French army band played "The Star-Spangled Banner" over and over again. Women ran alongside the marching troops to throw rings of flowers around their necks.

The column made its way to Picpus Cemetery. Here was buried the Marquis de Lafayette, the French nobleman who had fought with the Americans in the Revolutionary War.

A great crowd watched in tense silence as Pershing stepped forward and laid a wreath on the grave.

Then an aide, Colonel Charles E. Stanton, saluted and exclaimed, "Lafayette, we are here!"

It was reported at the time that Pershing had made the ringing statement, but the person was actually Stanton.

Pershing knew that the "Tommies," the British troops, were not as impressed with the new arrivals as the French people were. "Eleventh-hour soldiers," the Tommies called the Yanks, meaning that they had come in at the end of the war.

Inspections kept the American forces battle-ready.

Pershing told his staff, "Let's show the world what the eleventh-hour soldiers can do."

He knew that the eleventh hour was rapidly approaching. The Allies were trying to hold their lines until the Americans were ready for combat. Meanwhile, the Germans were trying to smash through to victory before the Yanks arrived in sufficient numbers to turn the tide of battle.

Slowly but steadily the American Expeditionary Force began to build up in France. Pershing constantly inspected his troops with the eye of an eagle. If a soldier in the rear ranks had a dirty rifle or a flap of his uniform unbuttoned, Pershing spotted it. That man was severely punished.

"There's one thing I can't understand about Pershing," Secretary of War Baker once remarked. "How can a man who worries so much about buttons be such a great general?"

Attention to such little matters was part of Pershing's West Point discipline. He wanted his men so highly trained, toughened, and sure of themselves that they could meet the excellent German army on equal terms—meet it and beat it.

In his training, Pershing stressed *attack* instead of the *defense* tactics favored by the British and French. He drilled his men in quick, slashing movements. He showed them that, when a position was strongly held, they could slip around the side and cut it off. As much as anything else, he worked on his troops' marksmanship.

"Gentlemen," he told his staff, "I want the American soldier to be the best shot in the world."

For weeks the Yanks drilled beyond the sound of the guns under British and French instructors. Then they were moved in companies and battalions to quiet sections of the Allied line, where they learned to live in the trenches. After that they were brought into more and more active sections.

Day and night Pershing roared around in his command car, Daisy, racing from one unit to another. Once Colonel Charles G. Dawes went with him. Like

Pershing, Colonel Dawes had suffered a personal loss. Before the war, his son had been drowned.

"Neither of us was saying anything," Dawes reported later, "but I was thinking of my lost boy and of John's loss and looking out the window. And he was doing the same thing on the other side of the automobile. We both turned at the same time and each was in tears. All John said was, 'Even this war can't keep it out of my mind.' "

As usual, winter's slashing rains and blinding snows brought a lull in the action. The Western Front was an ocean of mud, through which wagons and trucks and cannon could not be dragged. But Pershing continued to train the troops, anxious to have them ready for the major German offensive he knew would be coming with the first good weather in the spring. He also worked out the details of his battle plans, holding as many as twenty important conferences a day.

With all his labors, Pershing found time almost every evening to be tutored in French. He also managed to keep in physical shape. One December morning, Colonel Dawes reported, he happened to look out his window. "There was Black Jack, clad only in pajamas and slippers, running up and down in the snow. I never saw a man more physically fit for his age."

Pershing was promoted to four-star general, a rank held up until that time by just four other Americans: George Washington, Ulysses S. Grant, William T. Sherman, and Philip H. Sheridan.

The American people were pleased with all that Pershing was doing. The French, however, were not happy. A few months earlier they had been shouting, "*Les Américains* have arrived!" Now they were asking, "Where are the Americans? Why aren't they fighting?"

That is what Marshal Ferdinand Foch wanted to know. A little man with a big walrus mustache, Foch was France's most powerful military leader. He and Pershing talked through interpreters at the American general's headquarters.

"General Pershing," Foch said, "we no longer have the men to replace our losses. We must have American soldiers to put into our ranks!"

Pershing quietly replied, "Sir, because of the French and the British losses, the time may come when the American army will have to do most of the fighting. It would be a grave mistake to give up the idea of building that army as rapidly as possible. And right now the men have not had enough training to go into action."

"They can be trained in action," Foch pointed out.

"Sir, that would be murder!" Pershing exclaimed.

Marshal Foch (left) and Pershing at Chaumont.

"General Pershing, war is murder," Foch said. "And if we don't get your troops, we will lose the war!"

"You shall get them, Marshal Foch," Pershing replied, "just as soon as they are ready to fight. You know as well as I that the French and British and Americans all have different ways of doing things. My men will fight better and suffer fewer casualties if they are commanded by their own officers."

The British also began to insist upon Yank replacement for their combat losses. But Pershing refused to be forced. He knew that the American people demanded that they have their own army in France.

72

He also knew that the British and French did not want an American army, fighting under its own flag. The Allies wanted American soldiers to fight under the flags of Britain and France.

Besides the terrible casualties that the Yanks would suffer, the morale of the troops — so vital in war — would be destroyed. For if a battle were won, the British and French would claim all the credit. And if a battle were lost, they would blame the Americans.

Some of Pershing's stormiest actions were fought across the conference table as the Allies continued to apply pressure for him to give up his troops.

Meanwhile, he moved his headquarters to Chaumont, a beautiful town in the hills of eastern France, near the front. When Christmas came, he sent this message to the AEF (American Expeditionary Force):

> "Hardship will be your lot, but trust in God will give you comfort. Temptation will befall you, but the teachings of our Saviour will give you strength. Let your valor as a soldier and your conduct as a man be an inspiration to your comrades and an honor to your country. Germany can be beaten, Germany must be beaten, Germany *will* be beaten!"

8. "All We Have Is Yours"

Early on the morning of March 21, 1918, Pershing drove through heavy fog to Marshal Henri-Philippe Petain's headquarters near the front at Compiègne. Petain, a tall, sad-faced man with a drooping white mustache, commanded the French forces on the Western Front. As the American and Frenchman were talking through their interpreters, a loud rumble came to them from the north.

"Cannon fire," Pershing said. "The German offensive has started."

Petain had a worried expression, as the booming grew louder.

"Marshal, I now have four divisions in France," Pershing told him. "Only one—the First—is completely ready for action, but you're welcome to it."

"Thank you, General," Petain answered without much enthusiasm. "I'll have to see how your men can best be employed."

The Germans forced the Allies steadily back. The enemy planned to separate the British and French armies, then concentrate on the British and wipe them out. After that the French could easily be defeated. The German commander, Field Marshal Paul von Hindenburg, bragged that he would be in Paris by April 1.

The German army continued to advance toward Paris. Soon their long range artillery began to shell the French capital.

On March 28, Pershing jumped into Daisy and roared off to Marshal Foch's headquarters at a chateau near the front at Clermont. Pershing knew that Foch was about to be named Supreme Commander of all French, British, and United States forces in France. Obviously, this was the person to whom he should speak. Pershing found Foch and a group of long-faced French officers in the garden. In that peaceful spot, it was hard to believe that a furious battle was then raging less than twenty miles to the northeast. At once Pershing began to give a speech he had memorized in French:

> "*Je viens pour vous dire que le peuple américain* . . . I come to tell you that the American people would consider it a great honor to put our troops on the firing line. Infantry, artillery — all we have is yours."

Foch was delighted; but, in another meeting a short time later, he remarked that the Americans would have to come into the ranks of the other Allied armies.

"No, sir," Pershing quickly replied. "The American army will fight as a unit."

"Your men are scattered over too wide an area," Foch told him angrily. "It would take them too long to get together at the front as a unit. They may arrive to find the British pushed into the sea and the Germans in Paris!"

"Sir, I'm prepared to take that risk," Pershing answered quietly. "We will only fight as a unit."

The British Tommies finally stopped the enemy, although at heavy cost. Then came a period of quiet as the Germans collected their men and equipment for an all-out assault upon the Western Front.

To throw the enemy off-balance, Pershing ordered his First Division to take the German-held village of Cantigny, 50 miles north of Paris. Gathering his officers together, he gave them a fight talk. Fists clenched, arms swinging, he exclaimed, "You are going to meet savage enemies flushed with victory. Meet them like Americans! You are leading men. Be an inspiration to them! When you hit, hit hard— and don't stop hitting. You don't know the meaning of the word defeat!"

Then he returned to headquarters to go on with his other tasks and to await news of the assault, set for May 28. That morning he paced back and forth in his office, swinging his muscular arms, clenching and unclenching his fists.

The First Division's assault upon Cantigny, although not a major campaign, was the first American offensive of the war. Pershing knew that its success would give the sagging Allied morale a great boost. If it failed . . . but it would not fail! He had drilled the men until the whole division worked as a team. The phone rang, and Pershing rushed to take it from an aide.

"Everything went according to schedule, General," the First Division commander reported excitedly. "We hit them with artillery, then charged up the hill and took the village. The Germans just counter-attacked, but we held!"

"Well done," Pershing said with a sigh of relief. "Well done!"

Later the phone rang again. Marshal Petain's interpreter sounded frightened. "General Pershing, the Germans have launched an attack on Paris!" he exclaimed. "They've just captured Chateau-Thierry!"

Pershing glanced up at his map. The village of Chateau-Thierry, on the Marne River, was less than 50 miles from the French capital.

"*Mon général*," the interpreter went on, "Marshal Petain asks me to tell you that the Germans have nothing ahead of them but flat ground and a broken French army. The Marshal says you must release your soldiers to him or Paris will fall!"

Without hesitation, Pershing turned over the Second Division and part of the Third—even though the men were not completely trained for combat. They were rushed to Chateau-Thierry in trucks, cars, and buses.

Singing "Hail, hail, the gang's all here!" the Americans raced down the road. They passed long lines of retreating French soldiers, so tired they could hardly walk. When the French saw the singing troops, they began to shout, "*Les Américains* have come! They have come!"

The Germans did not realize that fresh troops had

The 37 mm gun weakened the entrenched Germans.

entered the front line. Confident of victory, they charged. Yank machine gunners and riflemen kept up a deadly fire, hurling the enemy back with heavy losses.

Northwest of Chateau-Thierry was a patch of forest called Belleau Wood, scattered with boulders and thick with underbrush. The Germans were there in strength. Petain ordered a brigade of 8000 American marines to attack.

The fighting was as furious as any seen in the war. The enemies battled from tree to tree, from boulder to boulder. The Germans had hundreds of machine gun nests, which the marines attacked with hand grenades, rifles and bayonets. When the last shot had been fired on June 25, Belleau Wood was a blackened ruin.

Nearly 1000 marines had been killed and more than 3000 wounded. But the brigade had captured the forest. The grateful French renamed the spot "The Wood of the American Marines."

"I could not be prouder of the men," Pershing told his staff. "They've shown the world how Americans fight. But for so many to die..." Sadly he shook his head.

A staff member remarked, "We must remember, General, what Napoleon said. 'It is just as impossible to win victories without loss of life as it is to make omelets without breaking eggs.'"

"I know," Pershing answered softly. "If we're not willing to accept casualties, this war could go on forever."

The seesaw fighting continued day by day, with neither side making any real gain. Then at midnight, July 15, Pershing was in his Chaumont headquarters when he heard the furious booming of cannon from the northwest.

"The Germans are attacking Chateau-Thierry again," he remarked to an aide.

Hindenburg had decided to gamble everything

on a massive assault, hoping to smash through the Allied line and win the war that summer. He had taken all his combat veterans under thirty years old from the rest of the Western Front and sent them to Chateau-Thierry.

The enemy barrage kept up until dawn. Then the German infantry began to cross the Marne River in boats, concealed by a smoke screen. But morning breezes blew holes in the thick white cloud. The Americans on the south bank of the Marne saw the waves of boats and opened fire.

Shells screamed down upon the river, throwing up huge fountains of water. Boats and men were tossed high into the air. Yank riflemen and machine gunners fired until their weapons burned their hands. Still the enemy came on.

"General, they've reached our side of the river!" an American officer reported on the field telephone. Over the static of the phone, Pershing could hear the hammering of machine guns, the sharp bang of rifles, and the crash of hand grenades.

"Tell the men they must stick to the death!" he shouted.

"Stick to the death!" The order went down the American line. Whole companies were wiped out, but the Yanks stuck. Once more they threw the Germans back.

Two days later, the Americans made a counter-attack. Fighting beside them was the famous French foreign legion. The two forces slammed into the Germans and pushed them steadily back, capturing many cannon and prisoners.

As the fighting raged in other places along the Western Front, Pershing lent more American divisions to the French and the British. Before the end of the month, the Allied armies—stiffened by the Yank units—had stopped the last German offensive of the war.

By then, 250,000 American soldiers were arriving in France every month, along with thousands of tons of equipment and supplies.

"It's time we fought under our own flag," Pershing told his staff. On July 24, he issued a general order announcing the formation of the First American Army, with himself as commander.

9. Over the Top at St. Mihiel

Pershing studied the map on his headquarters wall. The St. Mihiel Salient stuck into the Allied line like an arrowhead. Pershing smiled grimly. At last he could remove that arrowhead, for Marshal Foch had given permission for the First American Army to make an offensive.

The assault date was set for September 12. Pershing started to gather his divisions in front of St. Mihiel and moved into battle headquarters close to the salient. The French general, turning over command of the area, handed Pershing the French plan for military operations there. It was 300 pages.

Pershing's own battle plan was just fourteen pages. Even then he was worried that it was too long!

His staff met to discuss the campaign, and one of his aides outlined the battle plan to the others.

"This operation will be a tough one," the aide said. "The Germans have been fortifying the salient since the beginning of the war. Two major French offensives against it were thrown back with heavy losses."

"Because the French made a frontal assault," Pershing explained.

"The German trench system is from four to six miles deep," the aide went on. "If the front line is

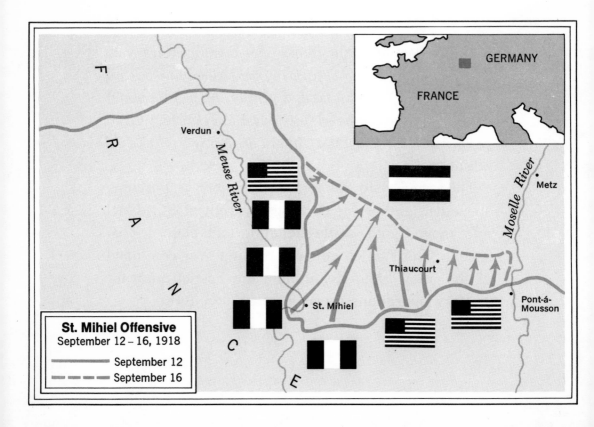

St. Mihiel Offensive
September 12–16, 1918

—————— September 12
– – – – – – September 16

taken, there's another after that—then another, and still another. The enemy has thousands of machine gun nests guarding the trenches. All their lines are protected by thick snarls of barbed wire."

Pershing nodded sadly. Barbed wire tore a man's flesh just as surely as bullets.

The aide pointed to a map. His yardstick touched the middle of the salient, where the mountain of Montsec was indicated.

"From here," he told the group, "German artillery can rain fire down on the attacking troops."

"We won't send troops against the mountain," Pershing announced. "That would cost too many lives. We'll blast the mountain with artillery, then make separate drives from each side of the salient. The enemy will either have to retreat or be surrounded."

"General," one of the officers said, "the Germans know we're going to hit somewhere along the line. It would be good if we could fool them about the exact spot."

"You're right!" Pershing exclaimed.

At once he began to work out a plan. He sent some officers to Belfort, a tiny town on the Swiss border, where there were many German spies. The officers rented rooms in a Belfort hotel and put up a sign outside, saying, "Headquarters."

Pershing wrote orders for an offensive to be launched from Belfort, stamping them "Secret." He told one of the officers to leave them on the bed of his hotel room. When the officer returned to his room, the orders were gone.

The Germans moved three full divisions from St. Mihiel to guard against the American "offensive" at Belfort.

For the assault, Pershing had 550,000 American troops, along with some French support units. He continued to drill his men for the great offensive. Each man knew exactly what he had to do and by when he had to do it.

Bridges and roads had been built close to the front. Under cover of night, the guns were moved into place, and the tanks crawled into their jump-off positions.

Dumps for more than 3,000,000 shells were placed close to the cannon. Water and food for the troops were in good supply. Ambulances were ready to bring the wounded back to American field hospitals.

Then on August 30 Marshal Foch called at General Pershing's battle headquarters.

"I've changed my plans," he said. "I've decided to launch a major offensive on a 200-mile front from Rheims to the North Sea."

"Yes?" Pershing was filled with suspicion.

"So," Foch said easily, "we'll need most of the

divisions you have at the St. Mihiel Salient. They will be put under French command."

Pershing was furious. "Marshal Foch," he said, "almost on the eve of the American offensive, you ask me to give back my divisions. That would practically destroy the American army we've been trying so long to form!"

"I must insist upon the arrangement," Marshal Foch snapped.

"Marshal Foch," Pershing replied, "you may insist all you please, but I refuse to agree with your plan. Our army will fight wherever you decide, but it will not fight except as an independent American army!"

Red-faced, Marshal Foch grabbed up his papers and maps, then stalked out of the room.

Three days later he summoned Pershing to French headquarters, and the argument was continued. Foch was insistent, but Pershing refused to budge.

"Very well!" the Marshal said at last. "You may have your St. Mihiel operation. But only if you help in the general Allied offensive on September 25."

"What's my assignment?" Pershing asked.

Foch watched him closely. "The Argonne Forest."

Pershing's face remained like stone, but the news was a shock. He was to launch one offensive, then— less than two weeks later—launch another a full 60 miles away.

To do this, he would have to move all his troops, cannon, tanks, trucks, and supplies over three narrow roads. These could be used only at night to avoid enemy observation. The transportation difficulties were so serious that such an operation usually took, not weeks, but months of preparation.

"I agree," Pershing replied.

The night of September 11, he was at battle headquarters just behind the front lines, telephoning last-minute instructions to his units. Outside, through the steady drip of the rain, came the crunch of boots as the long columns of American troops moved up to the front.

Pershing hung up the phone and glanced at the clock. It was nearly 1:00 A.M.

"Almost time for the bombardment to begin," Secretary of War Newton D. Baker remarked. He had come over from the United States to observe the American offensive.

Pershing gazed across his desk at the other man.

"You know, Mr. Secretary, there's never been a battle in history in which everything went right," he remarked. "Mistakes are paid for in pain and death—and disgrace. I've done my best to see that we make the fewest mistakes possible. Well, soon we'll know how successful I've been."

The troops had passed. The only sounds were the ticking of the clock and the drip-drip-drip of the rain.

Then the air above headquarters was screaming with shells, as nearly 3000 cannon opened fire upon the German positions. The booming of the guns and the crashing of the shells rocked headquarters, making the maps on the walls flap like sails in a wind. The barrage roared on for four hours.

Pershing and Baker put on their trenchcoats and helmets. Then they went out into the rain and drove to a hill from which they could watch the battle. H-hour, the time set for the attack, was 5:00 A.M.

The eastern sky was exploding with star shells and red and green signal flares. Villages caught in the bombardment blazed like bonfires. The German positions were flashing with shell bursts.

Slowly dawn came — a wet, foggy dawn. Up ahead, whistles blew, and the men went over the top of their trenches, cheering. They pressed forward through the fiery mist, then scattered and took cover when they came to a machine gun nest. As riflemen kept the enemy gunners busy, other Americans crawled around to the side of the nest and threw grenades. Then they charged with fixed bayonets.

Tanks moved up, spraying the German positions with machine-gun fire. Behind the clattering steel monsters came more troops.

The artillery barrage had blasted big holes in the enemy barbed wire, but most of it was still in place. Some American soldiers crawled forward with wire cutters and snipped a path for the assault troops. Other Yanks carried Bangalore torpedoes, long metal tubes filled with explosive. Slipped under the barbed wire, the torpedoes exploded and blew the wire back on each side.

From his hill, Pershing could not see all this action and could only hope that the men were performing the way he had trained them. Leaving Baker on the hill, he returned to battle headquarters. Overhead, a steady thunder sounded as Allied pilots flew in to bomb and machine gun the enemy.

Tanks moved machine-gun fire up to the front.

"Sir," a staff member called when Pershing entered his command post, "all our units report they are advancing on schedule! Many are ahead of schedule!"

"Excellent!" Pershing said. "Tell them to keep driving in."

Shortly before noon, a carrier pigeon came fluttering into headquarters. An aide took the bit of paper from the little tube on its leg and brought it to his commanding officer. Pershing read the message and grinned.

"Gentlemen," he announced, "at eleven o'clock this morning the Second Division captured Thiaucourt!"

The staff cheered, for the village was an important objective.

Later that day Pershing again heard the tred of boots. Looking out, he saw long gray lines of enemy prisoners being marched to the rear. The next day the Yanks captured the whole St. Mihiel Salient.

President Woodrow Wilson sent a cable to Pershing: THE BOYS HAVE DONE WHAT WE EXPECTED OF THEM.

Foch also sent Pershing a message. He complimented him on his "magnificent victory by a maneuver as skillfully prepared as it was valiantly done."

Pershing gave his troops a well-deserved rest. For him, however, there could be no rest. He had to go on planning the new offensive—up to that time the greatest in American history.

10. The Bloody Argonne

Pershing and his staff pored over their maps of northeastern France. The Americans were assigned a 25-mile area from the Meuse River through the Argonne Forest.

"Foch has given us the toughest sector of the whole Western Front," a staff member growled.

"The French never even considered making an offensive there," another added. "They thought the German positions too strong. Look, the Argonne is no v-shaped salient like St. Mihiel. It's a straight front."

"Yes," Pershing said grimly, "we'll have to take it in a frontal assault."

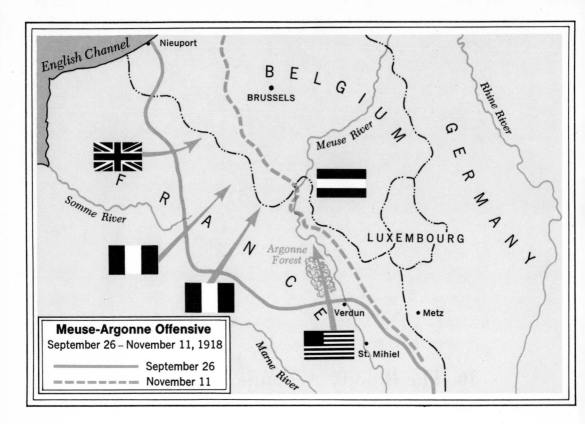

English Channel
Nieuport
B E L G I U M
BRUSSELS
Meuse River
Rhine River
G E R M A N Y
F
R
A
N
C
E
Somme River
LUXEMBOURG
Argonne Forest
Verdun • Metz
Marne River
St. Mihiel

Meuse-Argonne Offensive
September 26 – November 11, 1918
——————————— September 26
– – – – – – – November 11

The staff officers gazed at each other silently, aware that the frontal assault was the costliest of all attacks.

The mountainous forest was like a series of steps climbing upward, and ideal for defense. Thick belts of barbed wire stretched through the woods. Cannon and machine guns were hidden in deep holes. If Pershing's troops got past the first line of defense, there were many more just as strong.

The enemy had cut tunnels in the solid rock beneath the earth, to join one stronghold with another. Their dugouts were sometimes hundreds of feet down. There the German troops were safe from any barrage.

Pershing pointed to the railroad drawn on the map just behind the forest.

"That, gentlemen, is our objective," he announced. "That railroad is the enemy's main line of supply to the Western Front. When we capture it, all German forces in France will be cut off. Now, let's get to work!"

At night, the American troops moved up to take the place of French units in the Meuse-Argonne sector. By September 25 everything was ready; H-hour was 5:30 A.M. next day.

Pershing had moved his headquarters to a train hidden in the woods close to the Argonne Forest. The night of September 25, fog pressed against the windows like a thick blanket. At 2:30 A.M. the American cannon opened up all along the front, firing steadily until 5:30 A.M. Then whistles blew, and the Yanks charged forward.

Each American division had an objective for the first day's fighting. That of the Seventy-ninth Division was Montfaucon, a little village perched on the side of a mountain.

"It will take you all winter to capture Montfaucon," a French officer told Pershing.

"We'll see," he replied softly.

The Seventy-ninth fought hard all day but made little progress. Early the next morning Pershing got on the phone. He could barely hear the division commander's voice in the storm of exploding German shells.

"Take Montfaucon by one means or another!" Pershing shouted. "But take Montfaucon!"

On the following morning, September 27, the Seventy-ninth stormed into the village and pushed the enemy out. The Germans counterattacked with heavy artillery and machine gun fire. Then the Americans noticed a strange odor in the air. A low gray cloud was blowing toward them from the enemy position higher on the mountain.

"Gas! Poison gas!" the officers yelled to the troops. "Put on your gas masks!"

The Americans quickly obeyed, then opened fire on the Germans who came charging through the haze wearing their own gas masks. The fighting was vicious, and both sides took heavy casualties, but the Yanks held.

Pershing went up to the front. The forest was filled with the nervous chatter of enemy machine guns and the buzz of bullets. It seemed that his men had broken open a whole city of hornet nests. The Americans fell by the hundreds, but they kept climbing.

From high overhead came the roar and snarl of motors, as Allied and German planes engaged in dog-fights. An Allied plane fell out of the sky, smoke like a long black plume trailing behind it. A German plane went spinning down in flames. The war in the air, Pershing thought, was almost as furious as the one on the ground—*almost*.

He went from one division to another, drawing a circle on the map. "That's your objective," he told each commander. "Take it!"

One complained, "General, my men have been fighting for 48 hours straight. They're too tired to go on."

"I've had a look at your men," Pershing snapped. "I think it's you that's tired and not the men!"

He relieved some officers of their command and put in men with more energy and fighting spirit. The bitter work continued as the Yanks climbed the steep, rocky, muddy staircase of the Argonne.

A week went by. Once or twice the sun came out briefly but then hid behind the heavy clouds for good. A cold rain fell almost steadily. Supply wagons and cannon got stuck in the mud.

"Go through!" Pershing ordered his troops. "Go through!"

To his staff, he said, "If we strike hard enough, we may end this war in another couple of months. Otherwise, with winter coming, our attack is bound to get bogged down in the bad weather. Then the Germans could strengthen their lines to prepare for our spring offensive. The fighting might drag on through the

summer and fall of 1919 and thousands more men would be killed."

Elsewhere on the Western Front, the French and British were also attacking. But the Argonne was so important to the Germans that they took troops from other parts of their line and rushed them to the forest. Their orders were to stop the Americans—no matter the cost.

Still, week by bloody week, the Yanks kept advancing. Pershing studied his men. They were tired, hungry, red-eyed, and pale. So was he. His face was gray from the sunless days and his exhaustion. His shoulders slumped from lack of exercise. He squared them.

Rain-soaked soldiers march to the front along muddy roads (top left), move out of the trenches (bottom left), and maintain a continuous artillery barrage (below) in the final drive to win the war.

"Go through!" Pershing commanded. "Go through!"

The troops went through, taking ground and heavy casualties. Some divisions lost more men than the entire American army had at St. Mihiel.

"How hard it is to keep driving them in!" Pershing told his staff. "But this is war. It's the way to a quicker end, with less loss of life. I should fail in my duty if I didn't demand all that all of us can give at this time."

From across the Meuse River on the right, big German guns began to hurl shells at the Yanks. The bombardment was like a knife in the ribs.

An officer reported the situation to Pershing. "Sir, those guns on Hill 378 are raking us. We can't get our own guns up to silence them."

"I have no reserves to send across the river," Pershing said grimly. "The men will just have to take the fire."

The costly American advance went on. Then the Twenty-ninth Division came up to the line.

"Take Hill 378," Pershing ordered.

During the night American engineers built bridges over the Meuse, and the Twenty-ninth crossed the river. At dawn next day it stormed the hill. The Yanks took heavy losses, but after desperate fighting, they captured the hill.

By the end of October, the Americans had advanced five miles through the forest. The Argonne was a

100

nightmare scene of torn trees and tortured earth. Every day, however, the number of German prisoners increased.

By now, over 1,700,000 Yanks were engaged in the Meuse-Argonne offensive. Yard by yard, they battled their way to the top of the hills.

One day early in November, the phone at headquarters rang, and an aide answered. "General!" he shouted. "Our forces have captured the railroad!"

The command post was filled with cheers. Staff members slapped each other on the back and rushed up to Pershing with their hands outstretched. Pershing smiled, shaking hands all around. After more than 40 days of desperate fighting, the end was in sight. He cabled Baker at the War Department that the Americans had cut the enemy's main line of communications. Nothing but surrender or an armistice could save the German army from complete disaster now.

The reports continued to come into headquarters. The Yanks had captured 874 cannon and more than 3,000 machine guns in the campaign. They had inflicted about 100,000 casualties upon the enemy, but 117,000 Americans had been killed or wounded.

Pershing shook his head sadly, remembering what Napoleon had said about victories and omelets. The difference was that men were not eggs.

Pershing was at his desk early the morning of November 11, 1918, when an aide rushed in. "Sir, Marshal Foch's headquarters just called. Germany has surrendered! The war is over!"

Pershing leaned back in his chair, hearing the cheers as the news spread. Car horns were honking, and in a nearby village the church bell began to chime. "Thank God," he sighed. "Thank God!"

"The cease-fire is set for 11:00 A.M. today," the aide went on.

"The eleventh hour of the eleventh day of the eleventh month," Pershing remarked softly. "I wonder what the world thinks of America's 'eleventh hour soldiers' now?"

Then, as other generals rushed off to take part in the wild victory celebration in Paris, Pershing went right on working at his desk.

11. Homeward Bound

The war was over, but Pershing still had a mountain of work to do. He had brought 2,000,000 American soldiers to France. Now it was his job to get them home.

Everyone wanted to go home right away. This, of course, was impossible, and Pershing had to see that the morale of the men did not suffer as a result.

It was a hard job and one for which the homesick men did not thank him. But Pershing had done many hard, thankless jobs before. And now he was no longer so lonely, for young Warren had come over to be with his father.

"Sergeant" Warren Pershing with the staff in France.

Warren was now ten. He had blond curly hair and looked much the same as Pershing had looked in earlier years.

Pershing was proud of the boy. He dressed him in a sergeant's uniform and took him along wherever he went.

Once, when Pershing's command car was driving along a country road, it came upon a group of French people trudging home to their shell-torn farms. When they saw Pershing in the car, the people began to cheer. Pershing stopped the car and stepped out.

"You will rebuild better than before," he told the

people in French. "Clear your fields and have a good harvest. But be careful of shells that have not exploded."

"*Oui, mon général*," the French said. "We will. Certainly! Absolutely!"

Pershing waved good-bye and climbed back into the command car. He spoke softly to his driver, so that Warren could not hear. "How long before their new homes will be smashed in another war?" he asked sadly. Then he said, "But that is for the statesmen to decide."

President Woodrow Wilson came over to France for the peace talks with the other statesmen of Europe. He ate Christmas dinner with Pershing at his old headquarters at Chaumont. Pershing and the President inspected the quarters of the Twenty-sixth Division. On each man's bunk his equipment was laid out, every article in a special place.

"What's that?" Wilson asked, pointing to a short pole.

Pershing picked it up and handed it to the President.

"That, Mr. President, is a pole for a pup tent," he said.

Wilson studied the pole a moment. Then he handed it back to Pershing, who tossed it back on the bunk.

"What if that man's bunk were inspected again?" the President demanded. "He would get into trouble.

As your commanding officer, I order you to put the pole in its proper place."

Pershing's face got red. After all, he had commanded the greatest army the United States had ever put into the field. But he snapped to attention, saluted, and put the pole in its proper place.

President Wilson went on to Paris for the peace talks, and Pershing continued with his own work. Finally his job was finished.

On the afternoon of September 1, 1919, Pershing and Warren were taken by launch out to the ocean liner *Leviathan*, anchored in the harbor of Brest, France. With them was Marshal Foch.

The two men stood together on the deck of the ship, their eyes glistening with tears of emotion. Sea gulls swarmed overhead, screaming. The *Leviathan's* horn gave a long, hoarse blast.

Pershing and Foch shook hands. Then, in the French fashion, Foch hugged Pershing and kissed him on both cheeks. The Marshal climbed down to the launch. Pershing stood at attention, saluting his old commanding officer, and Foch returned the salute as the launch roared off.

Then Pershing stood with his arm around his son. The *Leviathan* slid through the flashing water of the harbor toward the Atlantic Ocean, America, and home.

12. Taps

On board ship, Pershing received a radio message saying that Congress had made him General of the Armies. He knew that the only other man in American history to have been offered this rank was George Washington.

When the *Leviathan* entered New York Harbor on September 9, all the ships in port blew their whistles and sirens. The next day, Pershing led the First Division down Fifth Avenue, and the cheers of the people nearly drowned out the bands. Pershing grinned broadly when his excited horse broke into a trot.

After their vacation together, Warren went back to school in Lincoln, Nebraska, and his father returned

Pershing reviews returning troops in New York City.

to Washington for his new duties as Chief of Staff. Under his direction, commanders of regiments, divisions, and larger units went to war schools. There they studied the best ways of fighting a war, if it came.

"I want to be sure that the United States is prepared to fight, as we were *not* when we entered the last war," Pershing explained.

On September 13, 1924, his sixty-fourth birthday, Pershing retired from the army since retirement at his age was the army rule. The following year, as a special ambassador, he visited most of the countries of South America. Then he went to France, where he saw that the cemeteries of American soldiers who had given their lives in the war were made attractive spots.

As head of the American Battle Monuments Commission, he ordered that monuments be built at Belleau Wood, Montfaucon, and other places where the Yanks had fought.

He also wrote his memoirs, *My Experiences in the World War*. In 1932 the book received the Pulitzer Prize, a high literary honor.

On summer vacations, Warren often traveled with his father. Pershing had wanted his son to go to West Point, but Warren did not care to be a soldier. Though Pershing was disappointed, he said nothing. Warren went to Yale University, where he was voted the most popular man in his class. After graduation, he began a successful business career in New York City.

As Pershing grew older, he had to give up horseback riding. He still went for long walks in Washington's parks, but now younger men could keep up with him. He read a good deal, particularly books of action and adventure.

Sadly, he watched while Europe moved toward another great war. He was sure that the United States would be drawn into the fighting.

In September, 1939, World War II broke out in Europe. Then on December 7, 1941, Japanese planes bombed Pearl Harbor, the United States naval base in Hawaii. America was in the war.

Dressed in a neat blue suit, Pershing went to see President Franklin D. Roosevelt at the White House.

"Mr. President," he announced, "I've come to offer my services to my country."

"General Pershing," Roosevelt replied, "you are magnificent!"

But Pershing was eighty-one years old and in poor health. He could only sit on the sidelines and watch.

When Warren enlisted in the army, Pershing was delighted. Warren asked his father not to use his influence to help him in the army, and Pershing agreed. Warren worked his way up from private to major. He took part in the invasion of Normandy, France, and the rest of the fighting in Europe.

"He doesn't say much about himself," Pershing remarked, "but I think he's making a good soldier."

Pershing's health continued to decline, but he saw the United States through to victory in 1945. Then on July 15, 1948, just short of his eighty-eighth birthday, Pershing died.

He lies buried in Arlington National Cemetery in Washington, D.C., under an enlisted man's marker, as he had requested. His final wish was: "When the last bugle is sounded, I want to stand up with my soldiers."

Index